Old Eston & Normanby

Paul Chrystal

Eston, High Street.

This is how in 1870-72, John Marius Wilson described Eston in his *Imperial Gazetteer of England and Wales*: ESTON, a village and a chapelry in Ormsby parish, N. R. Yorkshire. The village stands on the ascent of Barnaby-Moor or Eston-Nab, near the Middlesborough and Saltburn railway, 2 miles S of the estuary of the Tees, and 5½ NW by W of Guisborough; and has a post office under Middlesborough, and a station with telegraph on the railway. … The chapelry comprises 1,919 acres of land and 835 of water. Real property, £23,508; of which £18,450 are in iron-works. Pop. in 1851, 465; in 1861, 2,835. Houses, 518. The increase of population arose mainly from the opening of extensive ironstone works, and the establishment of blast furnaces. The property is much subdivided. Eston-Nab is a detached hill, 784 feet high; has remains of an ancient camp; commands a fine prospect; and possesses interest in great modern quarries and ironstone pits. The living is a p. curacy, annexed to the vicarage of Ormsby, in the diocese of York. The church is good.

Text © Paul Chrystal, 2019.
First published in the United Kingdom, 2019,
by Stenlake Publishing Ltd.
Telephone: 01290 551122
www.stenlake.co.uk

ISBN 9781840338393

**The publishers regret that they cannot supply
copies of any pictures featured in this book.**

Further Reading

Armstrong, E. *Normanby's Trilogy: The Mill, the Brewery, the Poverina*, Normanby 2010
Cleveland Federation of Women's Institutes, *The Cleveland Village Book*, Newbury 1991
Fairbrass, S. *A Factual Description of Normanby 1050-1901*, Normanby
Hardwick, S. *Further Memories of Normanby*, Normanby 2006
Hardwick, S. *Normanby Remembered*, Normanby 2005
Wardell, J.W. *The Economic History of Tees-side*, Yarm 1960

New Bank, Eston. Henry Bolckow, mining engineer John Marley and businessman John Vaughan discovered the main seam of ironstone on the Eston hills as they walked up the Lazenby Bank cart road. The Eston mine opened in January 1850 and remained operational for the next 99 years. Within 20 years Cleveland was the iron-producing capital of the world with over 40 pits operating and over a hundred furnaces belching fire along the Tees. By 1879 Eston was yielding over a million tons annually from its shafts and tunnels. It was the biggest mine in the area, producing 63 million tons. The seam in places was up to seven metres thick. It was also the most dangerous mine with over 300 recorded fatalities. Between 1801 and 1951 Stockton's population increased from 4,177 to 74,000 which is an eighteen-fold increase; Eston saw a 63 times increase from 530 to 33,300 (the population of Eston in 1851 was 1,000) while Middlesbrough showed an astonishing 6,000 times increase from 25 to 147,300.

New Bank, Eston. 1850.

New Bank Incline was built in 1853 to transport ironstone down from the open drift mines and quarries to the tipping yards at Eston. At the top there was a tramline that shipped the stone across the face of the hills from the various quarries and drifts down, via one of three inclines: Old, Trustee and New Bank, of which the latter was the steepest; by 1939 its work was over.

Last man, and horses, out of the Trustee Drift on the last shift in 1949. Production inevitably declined over time and had been falling since 1900. By the end of the 1930s the drifts and quarries around Eston and Normanby – Wilton Clay Drift, Lovell Hill, North Drift, Stable Drift, Quarry Siding, Agar's Drift, Lowthers Drift and New Bank – were all exhausted. The last wagons to New Bank set off just before the war in 1939. Only Trustee Drift at Eston remained but then only for another ten years. Over 63 million tons of ironstone had been mined; 375 men and boys lost their lives with many hundreds more suffering life changing injuries particularly with lost limbs, often dying prematurely.

Iron & Coal Trades Review 1937 told how the Eston Mines comprised Upsall and Chaloner Pits, both of which were worked by adits; there were two shafts, 556 ft. deep, at Upsall, one of which was upcast and the other used for pumping and winding men. Upsall Pit was opened in 1851, and was the first mine to be worked in Cleveland on an extensive scale… Chaloner Mine was three miles distant from Eston, and the ironstone was brought in train loads, or sets of 21 tubs, over the surface in three stages… The stone from Chaloner mine was passed over a screen at Eston to separate the fines, which were not calcined. Copyright © 1999-2018 by The Durham Mining Museum and its contributors.

Old Eston. With the discovery of ironstone in the Eston Hills thousands of workers flocked to the area, but there was, predictably, a housing shortage leaving the miners to find lodgings wherever they could, even in barns on local farms while some slept rough or in tents. Old Eston simply could not cope with the influx. New cottages were built east of the old hamlet of Eston. This new area of Eston was called California to reflect the 1849 Gold Rush in America and was built between 1850 and 1870 by Bolckow and Vaughan exclusively for their employees using sandstone quarried from Eston Nab. If you lost your job you had to move out.

OLD·ESTON

The oldest buildings are close to the Ship Inn and the blacksmith shop. California was built a mile east from there. South Eston was built around 1850-1880 in between the villages of Old Eston and California. The story of California is explored in *A Century in Stone* – a DVD by Craig Hornby charting the 'pilgrim workers who poured in for a stake in the great iron rush' and features archive film and interviews with the last of the mining community.

High Street with what looks like a funeral cortege drawing up. Eston Cemetery was established in 1863 and built as an extension to the church of St. Helen, which has since been dismantled and rebuilt at Beamish Museum. The cemetery contains the war graves of 55 Commonwealth service personnel of the First World War and 43 of the Second World War, including one unidentified Royal Navy sailor. St. Helen's started life as a 12th century chapel of ease. In 1545 it received its first priest, becoming a parish church in 1868 until it was superseded by All Saints in 1884.

In 1890 there were about 20 businesses on Eston High Street including drapers, grocers, a confectioner, a hotel, a butcher, a newsagent, an inn and various public services including a police station. John Trattles was postmaster at the post office, telegraph office and savings bank at 105 High Street around the same time. Services in Eston also included daily buses to South Bank Station and Middlesbrough, departing from the Talbot Hotel.

In this photograph High Street is devoid of all vehicles save for two pushbikes, allowing the children to pose for the camera in relative safety.

Jubilee Road was originally Bank Lane; the Golden Jubilee of Queen Victoria in 1887 triggered the change. Jubilee Road's most famous resident was the renowned opera singer, Elsie Maybelle McDermid who was born 19th July 1889. Around 1904 the family moved to a newly-built house on High Street which they named "Greenbank" which can still be seen. Elsie attended the County School in Eston till January 23rd 1905 when she graduated to Middlesbrough High School, a fee-paying school in those days. Newspaper reports dating from March 1906 tell of her singing at local charity events – many connected to Eston Congregational Church. The last event reported was at Middlesbrough Town Hall on 27th February 1911 and has her down as a "professional vocalist". After this she went to London where she studied under Nellie Rowe. Elsie's professional debut was at Covent Garden in 1914 where she had a minor role as a flower maiden in *Parsifal*. In December 1914 she joined the D'Oyley Carte Opera Company as a principal soprano and toured Britain till 1917 in leading roles. By 1920 she was with the Royal Opera, Covent Garden and performed in many operas for the company. In 1933 Elsie came back to "Greenbank" to recuperate from an illness but after a few weeks she died there on 2nd May 1933. She is buried in Eston Cemetery with other members of her family, but no headstone marks her grave.

Eston can boast two VCs: William Henry Short V.C. (1884-1916) – born and lived at 11, William Street, Eston, until the family moved to Grangetown in 1900. He played football for Grangetown Albion and Saltburn and Lazenby United Football Clubs and fought in the early stages of the battle of the Somme where he was killed showing gallantry and devotion to duty. His name is recorded on Grangetown War Memorial and the obelisk in Eston Cemetery. "He was foremost in the attack, bombing the enemy with great gallantry, when he was severely wounded in the foot. He was urged to go back, but refused and continued to throw bombs. Later his leg was shattered by a shell and he was unable to stand, so that he lay in the trench adjusting detonators and straightening the pins of bombs for his comrades. He died before he could be carried out of the trench. For the last eleven months he had always volunteered for dangerous enterprises, and had always set a magnificent example of bravery and devotion to duty". Short had worked as a craneman at Bolckow, Vaughan & Co Steelworks in Eston. Richard Douglas Sandford V.C. (1891-1918) – died as a patient at Eston Hospital 12 days after the Armistice and was buried at Eston Cemetery. He received the Victoria Cross for his gallantry in the Zeebrugge Raid in April 1918.

The Mining Institute or the North of England Institute of Mining and Mechanical Engineers, is an organisation dedicated to mining engineering, mechanical engineering, mining electrical engineering and related professions. It is the world's oldest professional mining organisation. The Eston institute in High Street opened in 1902 and was built of red brick at a cost of about £1,700. It comprised recreation and reading rooms and a five table billiard room. It was enlarged in 1908, at a cost of £600. 1d was docked from the miners' pay to pay for the upkeep.

The Miners' Institute saw the premier, to 400 guests, of Craig Hornby's *A Century in Stone* – he describes it as 'This 2-hour documentary [which] tells their [the miners'] story combining dramatisation, virtual reality, rare archive film and candid interviews with the very last of the mining community. It is a digital monument for them and a cultural landmark for Teesside'. After 41 shows and an audience of over 4,000, it made history by being the first local film to open at a Teesside multiplex. It outsold all Hollywood competition during its first week. The story made national news and by 2005 *A Century In Stone* had made the journey to Australia for shows in Sydney, Brisbane, Melbourne, Newcastle and Perth.

PROCLAMATION GEORGE V - Esto...

The proclamation of George V's (1865–1936) accession to the throne in May 1910 after the death of Edward VII, his father, earlier that year. The festivities are taking place outside the Miners' Institute in the High Street with Eston Miners' Old Brass Band there to provide the entertainment.

The Miners' Hospital was built by Bolckow & Vaughan in Eston High Street in 1884, originally for 20 mining casualties at a time – the two wards were, fittingly enough, named Bolckow and Vaughan – and had its own railway line to bring patients direct from the mines. The hospital later opened to the wider community and was enlarged in 1904, at a cost of £5,300, to accommodate 66 patients; X-ray apparatus was installed in 1911. It closed in 1980 and was demolished in 1981. However, the ironstone pillars at the gateway have been re-erected on the site.

The Miners' Hospital. Here is a small selection of the 375 men and boys who died in the Eston pits, some of them will have passed through the hospital: Bassett, Walter William, 22nd Mar 1911, aged 27, Miner, he was working with another miner in a broken working near the outcrop; the roof was of a clayey nature for a thickness of some 6 inches and had often to be taken down; some clay fell, and the deceased was coming out from the face when a further fall occurred and knocked him against the side of the place; this blow against the hard side fractured several ribs, causing them to pierce his right lung; he died later in the day in Eston Cottage Hospital. Fox, Ernest Alexander, 25th Sep 1903, (accident: 13th Sep 1903), aged 18, Driver, a tub, which had not been properly spragged ran down an incline and the horse he was driving saw it and turned out and crushed his finger between the timbers and side of place; tetanus set in and he died on the 25th. Large, Francis, 2nd July 1878, (accident: 26th June 1878), aged 23, Miner, both eyes destroyed and otherwise severely burnt by an explosion of powder while charging a shot hole. Smith, Eli, 8th Oct 1858, aged 42, he was engaged in barring a piece of ironstone down, when a large piece fell upon his head inflicting a compound fracture of the skull, breaking his neck, and completely smashing one of this arms, and thighs; he was killed on the spot, Buried: Wilton, St. Cuthbert on 10th Oct 1858.

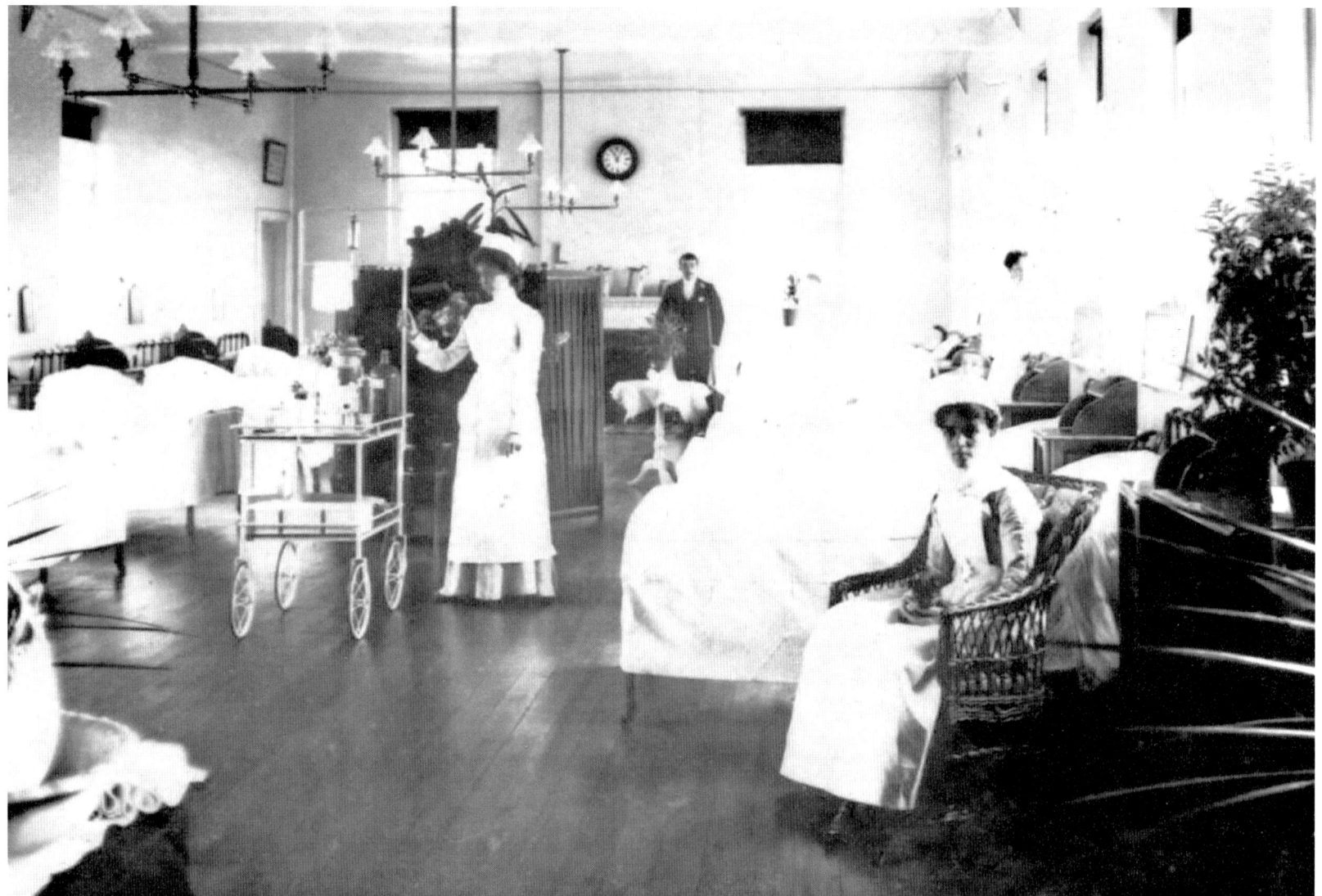

One of the wards in Eston Hospital around 1900.

The floating hospital at Eston jetty was set up to help deal with more than 800 cases of scarlet fever, enteric fever and smallpox in 1893. It came about because the situation locally had become so critical that the chairman of the Tees Port Sanitary Authority, Alderman Sadler, mooted the revolutionary idea of a temporary floating hospital on the Tees. It replaced the previous isolation hospital which from 1886 had operated from the brig *Remembrance* – maybe not the most hopeful or reassuring of names. Shipbuilders Head Wrightson won the contract and built a ship which accommodated 30 beds. Called *The Osprey*, it cost £800 and was in service until 1929.

The Primitive Methodist Chapel in Jubilee Street was erected in 1867, thanks largely to the beneficence of Mr. Elisha Beacham. It seated 700 persons and cost about £2,000. Adjoining the chapel were Sunday Schools and the chapel of the Bible Christians – a small structure built in 1884 seating 150. Eston has had six significant places of worship as well as a Salvation Army barracks.

The Evangelical Congregational Chapel was erected in Jubilee Road in 1858 with seating for 250 persons; an attached schoolroom was added in 1904. It was a substantial stone building in the Gothic style.

The Wesleyan Chapel was built in 1871 in the High Street at the junction of Church Lane opposite the Ship Inn, at a cost of £3,300. The foundation stone was laid by John Vaughan, then mayor of Middlesbrough. There was room for 500 worshippers, split between 74 pews to rent for 266 persons and a large gallery that could accommodate 226. Underneath there was a schoolroom for 300 children. The Home Guard used the chapel in the Second World War. Woodworm in the roof finally did for it and the chapel was demolished in 1959. Before the Wesleyan Chapel was built, the congregation worshipped in a chapel on Hewley Street. This older chapel, the California Chapel, was probably erected around 1854 when Lady Hewley's Trust leased them the land but refused to give money for building. The Church of England Christ Church can be seen in the background.

CHURCH AND VICARAGE
ESTON

Christ Church, the Church of England church is a traditionally designed red brick church which features sixteen stained-glass windows themed around saints. It was built in 1883 at a cost of £5,000 and consists of a chancel, nave with clerestory, aisles, south-west porch and an incomplete tower at the south-west angle, containing one bell. There are sittings for 500 persons. Today it is Christ Church, Eston, with Saint George's, Normanby – a joint parish of two churches. The vicarage house, opposite the church, was built in 1898.

The ancient church of St. Helen's goes back to 1100 and started life as a chapel of ease, getting its own priest in 1545. The church comprised a chancel and nave and an embattled western tower. It became the parish church from 1868 to 1884 when Christ Church was built. By 1998 the church had been languishing in disrepair for around 15 years and had been repeatedly wrecked by fire, partially demolished by vandals and the vestry had been stolen in its entirety. Despite being a Grade II listed building, permission was granted for its demolition until Beamish Museum stepped in at the last moment to rescue it. They carefully deconstructed the entire building stone by stone for rebuild and refurbishment on the museum site next to Pockerley Old Hall. It was opened to the public on 15th November 2015.

Eston Railway Station (seen here in 1906) was an NER passenger station between 1902 and 1929 and a goods-only station until 1966. It was the terminus of a short spur that curved east from the Normanby Branch of the Middlesbrough and Redcar Railway (now the Tees Valley Line). This was the second station to bear the name Eston. The original Eston Station closed on 22nd November 1885 and was replaced by South Bank Railway Station on a nearby site not actually in Eston but located two miles north in the South Bank.

The second Eston Station was on Station Road off Eston High Street. It gave direct access to the centre of Eston and the mining community of California (also called South Eston). It consisted of a single platform with a modest one-storey wooden station building and a coal depot behind. By 1911 it served a population of 28,095 people. Goods traffic was dominated by bricks, of which 6,416 tons were transported that year. However, the station was not heavily used by passengers. The number of tickets issued in 1911 was only 46,732 (about 128 a day). By 1925 there were only four trains per day each way, with a fifth on Saturdays, taking about 15 minutes to travel to and from Middlesbrough. The coal depot is on the right with piles of timber.

Normanby

Pony and trap in Cleveland Street outside the Methodist church in Patten Street, with Normanby corn mill in the background. Normanby had a state of the art corn mill – brick-built, steam-driven and four storeys high. The mill was operational from July 1875 and auctioned off in 1905. Horatio Taylor lived in Normanby Mill; he was a blacksmith and corn grinder – tragedy struck the family when one of his children aged three years was burnt to death in 1891.

The Eston & Normanby Social Club was built around 1856 and was originally the Oddfellows Hall. Oddfellows is an international fraternity first recorded in London in 1730. They espouse philanthropy, the ethic of reciprocity and charity. Increased trade during the Middle Ages led to guilds grouping people from a number of trades together. Hence, people of an odd assortment of trades may have formed the early Oddfellows.

Buxton's grocery shop at the corner of Mason Street and Lambton Street was owned by the Buxton family and run by James Buxton. The family business moved to Cleveland Street before Amos Hinton took over the premises and moved it to Lenny's Cafe in Normanby Road. The earliest mention of Normanby comes in 1823 in the *Directory of Yorkshire*. It describes Normanby in the Wapentake of Langbargh with a population of 122 including William Ward Jackson at Normanby Hall, Dorothy Jane Lambton, gentlewoman, four farmers, a victualler at the Bay Horse and a joiner. John Marius Wilson's *Imperial Gazetteer of England and Wales*, 1870-1872, describes Normanby as 'a village and a township in Ormsby parish, N. R. Yorkshire. The village stands 2 miles (3.2 km) N E of Ormsby r. station, and 4 W N W of Guisborough; and has a post-office under Middlesbrough. The township extends to the coast; and comprises 1,343 acres of land, and 355 of water. Real property, £7,949; of which £4,060 are in iron-works. Pop. in 1851, 195; in 1861, 2,204. Houses, 397. The increase of pop. arose mainly from the opening of extensive ironstone works, and from the establishing of glass furnaces. Normanby Hall is a chief residence. Bricks and tiles are made. There is a national school. Jackson owned most of the 1640 acres in 1840. In 1869 the main crops were wheat, barley, beans and clover.'

Lambton Street around 1910. All of these terraces were demolished in the 1920s to allow the link road between Cleveland Street and West Street, although the Lambton Arms – later The Tiger, and now The Lambert (after owner Jill Lambert) – survives. In January 2019 Jill Lambert commissioned David Earl to airbrush some iconic Teesside places on the walls of the pub, including Normanby Ironstone Mine, the blast furnace, Newport Bridge, Eston Nab, The Bottled Note, Ayresome Park, Riverside Stadium, and Roseberry Topping. Other pubs in the early 1900s included the Cleveland Hotel, Poverina Hotel, and the Woodman Arms on the corner of High Street and Lambton Street. The Poverina, first recorded in 1717, and Woodman are still serving today. William Wyrill was the village policeman in 1891, later posted south to Swainby. Jerome Delicate, chemist, made his own medicines in Lambton Street while Sandy Russel and his wife ran the post office. Ken Surtees ran a card shop.

Normanby High Street around 1920, with boot shop and grocers on the right and gable-end advertising on the left for Upton's and Rex Motors. Upton's started as a grocer's in South Bank in 1869, later moving to Nelson Street and becoming a household name around Middlesbrough. Eventually there were five branches in the area selling everything from radios and TVs, furniture to musical instruments. Upton's are noted for pioneering hire purchase. Other businesses included the Almond brothers' coal yard at the top of Cleveland Street, the Cleveland Inn, and the Bridal Workshop run by Sylvia Fairbrass. Jack Palmer sold newspapers from his house in Mason Street opposite the brewery.

High Street with The Woodman Arms, a popular two roomed pub famous for its home-made chicken curry and chips, on the left set back at the end. Other businesses on the High Street down the years include: the tobacconists and sweet shop (Connie's) run by Bill and Connie Buxton in the 1950s and 60s; the chip shop run from the front room of one of the houses using coal-fired pans – it later became Heward's cobblers; Bart Hogson's barbers on the corner of Parrington Street, later taken over by Charlie Simmons then Wilf White and his daughters Barbara and Sylvia; Bailey's (later Bentley's) cake shop between Parrington and Cleveland Street; Harrison's bike shop; Jane's the florist; Joe Redding's general store and bike repair shop; and Hawke's clothing and outfitter's shop on the corner. In the now-gone Laird Street and Dixon Street Miss Blake baked and sold her Christmas and wedding cakes and funeral teas, while 'Kipper' Heath sold his hot peas and ice creams. Further down was Harry Sisson's butcher shop, eventually taken over by Bernard Mazetti and then Bill Waddington. Sisson's slaughterhouse was at the end of Garden Place.

Above: Leggett's was a dairy shop run by Benny Leggett, milkman. Next door to Leggett's was a butcher who sold duck and peas.

Right: The Cleveland Hotel, now the Cleveland Inn, in Cleveland Street with patrons at the door and at the window. In 1897 five year old Winnifred Tratthen of Lambton Street was murdered by Thomas Edward Lloyd Cheney, son of Thomas Cheney the landlord of the Cleveland Hotel. He was detained in an asylum following his trial at Leeds Assizes.

The Poverina ('poor little thing'). At one time it was called the Bay Horse but owner William Ward Jackson of Normanby Hall renamed it after his favourite mare on the 6th February 1840. When he bought her she had been in a terrible state – emaciated with a broken knee – but gradually improved. Around 1925 the original Poverina was knocked down and the present building built in its place. While building work was going on the pub continued its trade in a disused railway carriage in a field alongside.

Hawkes outfitters shop in the early 1950s on the corner of Cleveland Street and the High Street. In the Second World War the proximity of Normanby and Eston to Middlesbrough and its own industries made the area a prime target for German bombers. The Eston Urban District area suffered 480 air raid alerts with 22 occasions when bombs were dropped. 107 high explosive bombs fell on the town and 489 incendiary bombs. 33 people were killed, 24 seriously injured and 67 slightly injured. 2,212 properties were damaged, of which 53 had to be demolished.

In the 19th century infanticide, usually by mothers, was relatively common, for all sorts of social reasons. In 1876 seventeen year old Annie Elizabeth Parker of Swan's Cottages in Normanby, stood trial for murdering her baby daughter. Her mother, Eliza, suspected that her daughter was pregnant – which Annie denied; when the girl complained of pain, her mother prepared a dish of mustard and water so that she could soak her feet. Eliza then went out to visit a neighbour. When another neighbour, Elizabeth Osbourne, heard a groaning noise coming from the privy, she called on Elizabeth Walker to go with her to the privy to investigate. There they found a baby girl lying face down; they took her into Annie's house where they established that the baby was in fact Annie's; she was sent to her room and a doctor was called. The baby's right arm appeared to be broken and there was a gash on the corner of her mouth. The doctor established that Annie had just given birth and that the baby was dead. A post-mortem revealed that the baby's arm was in fact broken, as if by a tight grip and that the mouth wound extended internally and had separated the windpipe and gullet from their structures; the jaw was also broken and there were abrasions on the body. An instrument had been used to cause these injuries which had taken place post partum. The birth, it turned out, took place in the kitchen as did the fatal injuries; marks were found on the privy wall which suggested that the baby had been dashed against the wall. The jury returned a not guilty verdict and Annie was discharged, despite the damning evidence against her. What she did have on her side, though, was her youth.

Normanby Bridge mishap. This incident took place in 1964 under the bridge over the road from Normanby to Ormesby carrying trains from South Bank to Eston via Normanby. It survives as a pedestrian bridge.

Normanby Bridge. No problem for this horse and trap getting under the bridge some years earlier.

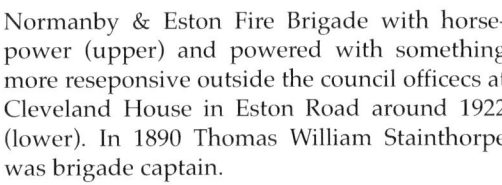

Normanby & Eston Fire Brigade with horse-power (upper) and powered with something more reseponsive outside the council officecs at Cleveland House in Eston Road around 1922 (lower). In 1890 Thomas William Stainthorpe was brigade captain.

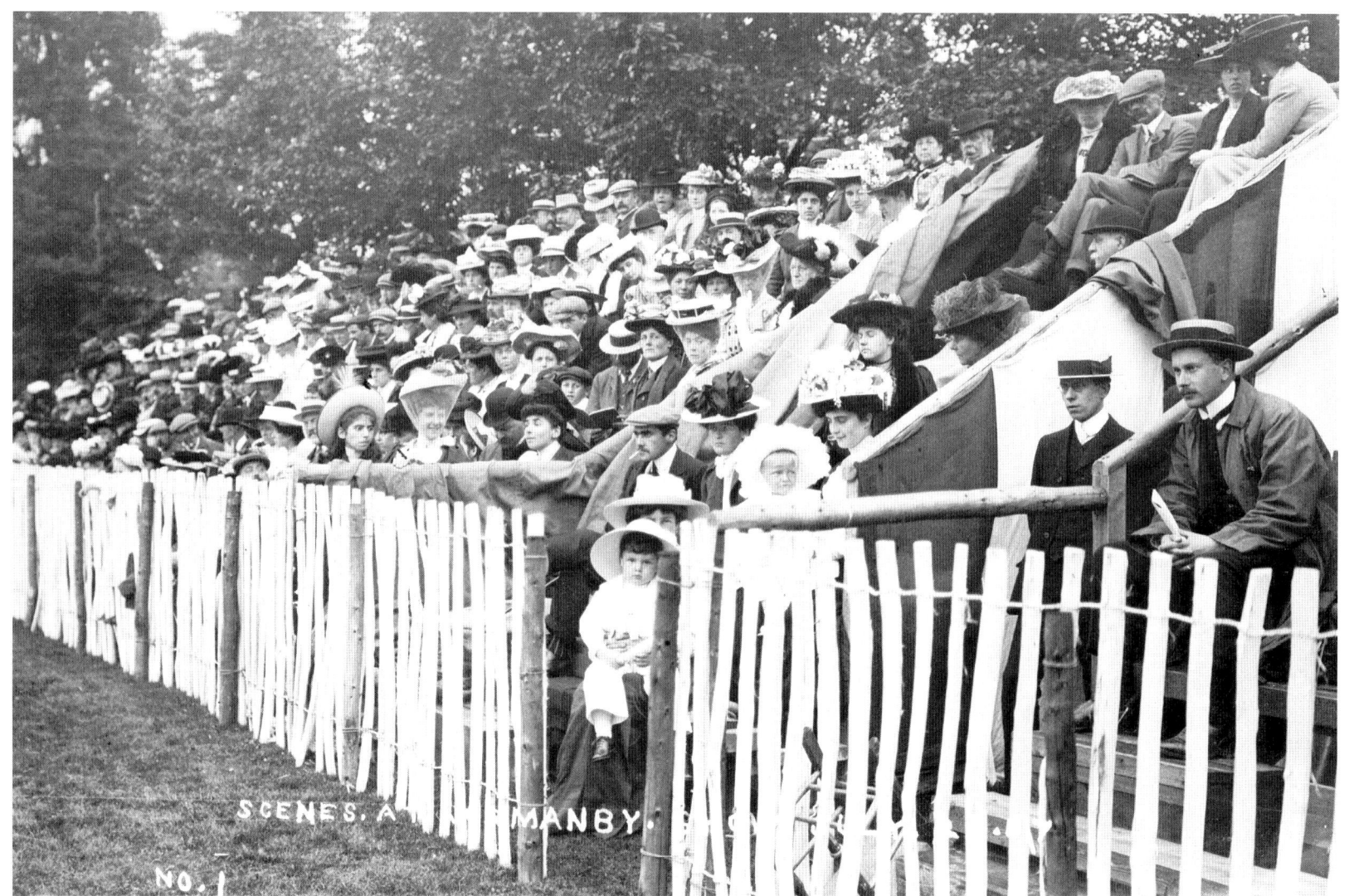

'Scenes at Normanby Show 1907' in Normanby Park, the annual summer carnival with fancy dress, Carnival King and Queen (both men), decorated tradesmen's traps and Eston Miner's Band. The parade finished at Jack Richardson's field near the signal box at Flatts Lane level crossing.

The Normanby Brick & Tile Company started production in 1883 and was a major employer in the area. In 1918 the site was bought by the Cleveland Magnesite and Refractory Company who had purchased the neighbouring brickworks at Ormesby two years previously. This purchase doubled the company's production of silica bricks to around 120,000 per week. Until 1939 the two brickworks also produced roof tiles and chimney pots, but production was later restricted to refractory bricks for industrial use such as blast furnaces. In 1953 Cleveland Magnesite was bought out by Steetley; in 1971 the works at both Ormesby and Normanby were closed down. The Normanby site was demolished in 1979 and the site became Flatts Lane Woodland Country Park which opened in 1994.

Flatts Lane Signal Box. Eston had two railway connections running more or less parallel to each other about a mile apart: the Normanby Branch route to the west of Eston and the older Eston Branch Railway to the east, which had been opened in January 1851 by Bolckow Vaughan to transport iron ore from its mines in the Eston Hills. The Normanby Branch crossed Flatts Lane at this level crossing just north of the junction with Hollywalk Avenue. To the east of the crossing the line split three ways; a fork to the north-east went to a coal depot serving Normanby, the middle fork went on to Eston and the third fork went south-east to the brickworks of the Normanby Brick & Tile Co. The track bed of the spur from the Normanby Branch is now a footpath from the site of the old level crossing at Flatts Lane to Station Road in Eston. The Normanby Branch itself is also now a footpath, the South Bank Walkway, which links Flatts Lane Country Park to South Bank.

Normanby School. In 1879 the National School was described as a 'handsome Gothic structure' and Ward Jackson had added school rooms and a residence. In 1890 the teachers were accused of excessive corporal punishment, or according to the *North-Eastern Daily Gazette* of 5th December 1890, of 'cruelty to children'. Apparently, Mr. Hardiman's son was lying dangerously ill and the doctor was unable to say whether he would recover or not; the 7½ year old boy had come home feeling unwell after being struck on the head by a teacher.

Normanby Park opened in 1929 and was known locally as "Tittybottle" Park as wet nurses frequently brought babies there to feed them. There is a similarly named park in Redcar. The house in the centre of the photo was the caretaker's house. The lake was filled in in 2006.

Cleveland Street is in the centre of Normanby. In 1870–72, John Marius Wilson's *Imperial Gazatteer of England and Wales* describes Normanby as follows: 'Normanby, a village and township in Ormsby parish, N. R. Yorkshire. The village stands 2 miles (3.2 km) N E of Ormsby r. station, and 4 W N W of Guisborough; and has a post-office under Middlesbrough. The township extends to the coast; and comprises 1,343 acres of land, and 355 of water. Real property, £7949; of which £4,060 are in iron-works. pop. in 1851, 195; in 1861, 2,204. Houses, 397. The increase of pop. arose mainly from the opening of extensive ironstone works, and from the establishment of glass furnaces. Normanby Hall is a chief residence. Bricks and tiles are made. There is a national school.'

SANATORIVM. ESTON.112

Eston Sanatorium, Flatts Lane, Normanby, also known as Eston Urban District Council Sanatorium, Eston Infectious Diseases Hospital, and Normanby Hospital, opened in 1893 at a cost of £2,466 and specialised in the treatment of tuberculosis. Designed to hold 36 patients it had a disinfecting chamber, mortuary and an isolation ward. The patients photographed above are recuperating with a game of croquet on the lawn.

The story of Richardson's Brewery started in 1852 with William Husband, owner of the Globe Inn, Stockton. He bought the Normanby Great Pasture in 1857 and built a new brewery on the corner of Mason Street and Crossbeck Terrace – it was on the site of artesian wells to the west of Paddy's Row and north of Bulmer's Row. The brewery operated until 1872 when John Lister Richardson became the owner. He changed the business from brewing to 'Aerated Mineral Water' or Richardson's Lemonade. Their logo from 1890 was a greyhound, reflecting Richardson's love of greyhound racing. His sons took over the business after his death in 1891 and started to bottle Guinness and Bass in 1895. The brewery was demolished in 1979. Lister R. Coverdale, a motor trolley driver of Brewery House, Normanby, delivered mineral water for Richardson Brothers wholesale beer bottle and mineral water manufacturers; he is interesting because around 1916 he appealed against his conscription to the North Riding Appeal Tribunal on the grounds that he was doing work of national importance by delivering mineral water to army camps in the vicinity. His appeal was dismissed.